Jenny Vaughan

Wild Weather
BLIZZARDS

QEB Publishing

Copyright © QEB Publishing, Inc. 2008

Published in the United States by
QEB Publishing, Inc.
23062 La Cadena Drive
Laguna Hills, CA 92653

www.qeb-publishing.com

All rights reserved. No part of this publication may be reproduced, stored in a retrieval system, or transmitted in any form or by any means, electronic, mechanical, photocopying, recording, or otherwise, without the prior permission of the publisher, nor be otherwise circulated in any form of binding or cover other than that in which it is published and without a similar condition being imposed on the subsequent purchaser.

Library of Congress Control Number: 2008012591

ISBN 978 1 59566 586 7

Printed and bound in the United States

Author Jenny Vaughan
Consultant Terry Jennings
Editor Amanda Askew
Designer Mo Choy
Picture Researcher Claudia Tate
Illustrator Julian Baker

Publisher Steve Evans
Creative Director Zeta Davies

Picture credits (a=above, b=below, l=left, r=right)
Alamy 16 Alaska Stock LLC, 25b Visual Arts Library (London)
Corbis 1 Colin McPherson, 4 Doug Wilson, 5 Philippe Renault/Hemis, 8 Tim Davis, 10a Christophe Boisvieux, 10b Ashley Cooper, 12a A Inden/zefa, 13a Tannen Maury/epa, 13b Christopher Morris, 15a Bo Zaunders, 17a Johan Copes Van Hasselt/Sygma, 17b Bettmann, 19br, 20a Staffan Widstrand, 21a Tim Davis, 22b Layne Kennedy, 23a Tiziana and Gianni Baldizzone, 24a Blue Lantern Studio, 24b Bettmann, 25a Bettmann, 26 Bettmann, 27a Sandro Vannini
Getty Images 6 Hiroyuki Matsumoto, 9 Norbert Rosing, 15b David Trood, 29b Richard Olsenius
Photolibrary Group 20b Robert Hardin, 22a
Rex Features 12b SUNSET, 14 Asgeir Helgestad/ Nature Picture Library, 29a Sipa Press
Science Photo Library 7t NOAA, 19a Dr Juerg Alean
Shutterstock 11 Jakub Cejpek, 18 Lloyd Paulson, 19bl Flashon Studio, 21b Pawel Strykowski, 23b Clouston, 27b Sascha Burkard
Wilson Bentley Digital Archives of the Jericho Historical Society/snowflakebentley.com 7b

Words in **bold** can be found in the glossary on page 30.

Contents

What is a blizzard? 4

What is snow? 6

Where are blizzards most common? 8

Mountain snow 10

Getting around 12

Surviving a blizzard 14

Dangers to health 16

Dealing with snow 18

Plants and animals 20

Living with snow 22

Blizzard tales 24

Coping with blizzards 26

The changing climate 28

Glossary 30

Index 32

What is a blizzard?

A blizzard is a form of extreme weather, with high winds and heavy snow. Normal life may grind to a halt. Traveling may become impossible, and temperatures can be dangerously low. Even after it is over, a blizzard leaves behind large amounts of snow, often driven by the wind into heaps, called **drifts**.

WIND AND SNOW

A blizzard is more than just heavy snowfall—it is an especially violent snowstorm. The definition of a blizzard used in the United States is a wind of more than 34 miles an hour, with enough snow in the air to make it impossible to see for more than 490 feet. A severe blizzard has winds of more than 44 miles an hour with temperatures below 10 degrees Fahrenheit. There must also be so much snow in the air that it is impossible to see anything at all.

◀ When heavy snow falls, roads become icy and may even be blocked completely—causing long traffic jams.

▲ Quebec, Canada, lies under a blanket of snow. Although it looks beautiful, cold temperatures and heavy snow bring problems.

WHERE DOES THE WORD "BLIZZARD" COME FROM?

Blizzards have happened for centuries, but the word "blizzard" as a term for a violent snowstorm is quite new. Until the end of the 19th century, it was used to mean cannon shot or musket fire. Then, in the 1870s, a newspaper in Iowa first used it to describe a heavy snowstorm with violent wind. The snow does not actually have to be falling in a blizzard—it may have been lying on the ground, whipped up by the wind.

WEATHER AND CLIMATE

WEATHER is…
wind—movement of the air
visibility—how far we can see in the air
precipitation—rain, snow, or hail
temperature—how hot or cold the air is
(measured in degrees Celsius, °C,
or degrees Fahrenheit, °F)
CLIMATE is the average weather
a place gets over a long
period of time.

What is snow?

...made up ice **crystals** that form from **water vapor** high in the **atmosphere**.

HOW DOES SNOW FORM?

As air gets warmer, it rises, and cools. Water vapor in the air **condenses**, or changes into droplets of liquid water. High in the atmosphere, it is so cold that the water droplets freeze into tiny ice crystals in the clouds. More ice forms around these, forming larger crystals, or snowflakes. As these fall through the air, they partly melt and collide with each other, forming fluffy lumps of snow.

2 Water vapor cools and condenses into droplets of water

1 Water vapor rises

3 The droplets then freeze and fall to Earth as snow

▲ Tiny ice crystals form in the clouds. More ice forms around these, making snowflakes, which fall to the ground. If these fall through warm air, they melt and become rain.

▼ A blizzard in New York City. In heavy snow, getting around is almost impossible.

WHAT CAUSES SNOW AND BLIZZARDS?

When cold winds force warm air full of water vapor upward very fast, huge quantities of snowflakes form. These fall through the extremely cold air beneath them without melting, as dry, powdery snow. At the same time, the meeting of cold and warm air creates strong winds. The result is a combination of heavy snow and wind, called a blizzard. Even when the snow reaches the ground, it may be whipped up again, filling the air with snow.

SNOWFLAKES

There are several kinds of snowflake, depending on the conditions in the clouds where they form. Some are simple, six-sided forms, while others are more like tiny needles. The best-known are **dendrites**, which look like six-sided stars, flowers, or ferns. Others are small grains of ice, like frozen drizzle. Yet others are extremely small, six-sided plates that are found in the very cold north and south polar regions. They sometimes just hang in the atmosphere. They glitter in the sunshine, and are often called "diamond dust."

▼ Dendrites are six-sided crystals of ice. No two are ever exactly the same.

THE SNOWFLAKE MAN

Much of what we know about snowflakes was discovered by a Vermont farmer named Wilson Bentley (1865–1931). With little education, he became an expert on snowflakes. He photographed thousands of them, using a microscope and a camera. He discovered that no two snowflakes are ever exactly alike.

▼ Wilson Bentley became a world expert on the subject of snow and he developed a way of photographing magnified snowflakes. He obtained his first photographs of snowflakes in 1885.

Where are blizzards most common?

Blizzards are common in parts of the world where warmer air full of moisture is most likely to meet very cold wind. These places are in the far north and south of the world, and at high **altitudes**—high above **sea level**.

ANTARCTIC BLIZZARD

Inland, in the **Antarctic**, there is rarely heavy snowfall, but there are blizzards. This is because the winds are extremely strong and cold. They blow the snow that lies permanently on the ground into the air, creating blizzard conditions.

▼ Young emperor penguins huddle together to protect themselves from an Antarctic blizzard.

PREVAILING WINDS

The winds that blow over the Earth's surface tend to travel in the same direction and are called prevailing winds. For example, just north and south of the **tropics**, the prevailing winds are "westerlies" (from the west). Westerlies are fairly warm and carry a lot of water vapor. Near the poles, the prevailing winds are cold easterlies (from the east). In winter, the easterlies are icy and strong. If the easterlies force themselves southward, they force the warmer air of the westerlies upward, creating snow and even stronger winds—perfect conditions for a blizzard.

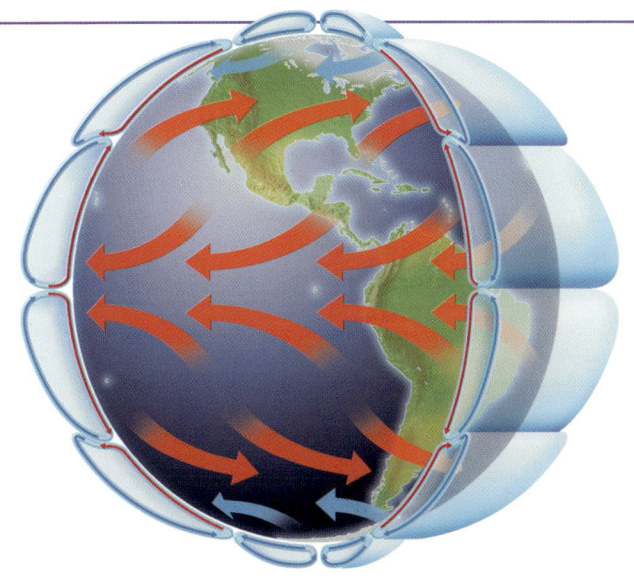

▼ Cold easterly winds travel around the Earth near the North and South poles. If they force themselves southward, they meet warmer westerlies, creating blizzard conditions.

THE HEAVIEST SNOW

Certain parts of the world, such as the Great Plains and the Great Lakes in North America, often have severe snowfall and high winds in winter. Northwest Europe, parts of Russia, Korea, China, and Japan also often experience blizzard conditions. People there know the kinds of weather that will lead to a blizzard. For example, in Russia, when a cold wind called the "Buran" blows eastward from the **Arctic**, a blizzard is expected.

◀ Musk oxen live in the cold regions of Alaska, Canada, and Greenland. Their thick winter coat protects them from the coldest winter temperatures.

9

Mountain snow

The air at high altitudes is cooler than it is nearer to sea level. As a result, snow is common on the upper slopes of mountains and on high **plateaux**.

AVALANCHE DEATHS
Between December 2005 and April 2006, 655 people died in avalanches in the French Alps—the highest number for more than 30 years.

◀ A powerful avalanche races down the slopes of Mount Pumori, in the Himalayan range between Tibet and Nepal.

◀ These fences have been put up to help hold back avalanches in winter.

MOUNTAIN DANGERS

Blizzards are extremely dangerous on mountains. Climbers may suffer from the severe cold and, if they cannot see properly, they may slip and fall. Another great danger comes from avalanches. These are massive, fast-moving masses of snow that slide down mountainsides. They happen most easily when temperatures start to rise after heavy snowfall. The new snow becomes unstable. The slightest movement—a skier on the snow, or even a loud noise—can start an avalanche. Snow tears down the slope, carrying rocks and ice and burying everything in its path. Anyone on the mountainside may be swept to their death, and buildings at the foot of the mountain can be buried.

▲ Climbers tread carefully on mountain slopes. Where there is a danger that they may slip, they will rope themselves together.

▼ The permanent snow line is the lowest point on a mountain above which there is always snow.

1 MOUNT EVEREST, NEPAL
2 MOUNT MCKINLEY, ALASKA
3 KILIMANJARO, TANZANIA
4 MOUNT COOK, NEW ZEALAND
5 GUNNBJØRN FJELD, GREENLAND

1 Height 29,028 feet Permanent snow line around 18,700 feet
2 Height 20,321 feet Permanent snow line around 7,000 feet
3 Height 19,340 feet Permanent snow line around 16,400 feet
4 Height 12,312 feet Permanent snow line around 5,900 feet
5 Height 12,139 feet Permanent snow line around 2,000 feet

THE SNOW LINE

The point on a mountain above which it is always snowy is called the **permanent snow line**. The altitude of this line varies according to where on Earth the mountain is, and the time of year. The warmer the sea-level temperature, the higher the snow line. Winds, temperature, and the amount of moisture in the air also affect the altitude of the snow line. The snow line on mountains in tropical regions can be as high as 18,700 feet, while in the Alps of Western Europe, it is about 6,500 feet above sea level. The snow line is actually at sea level in polar lands.

11

Getting around

Modern life can come to a standstill in a severe blizzard. High winds and heavy snowfall can bring down **power lines**, leaving whole communities without electricity. Travel may become impossible.

ROAD TRAVEL

Blizzards are extremely dangerous to anyone trying to make a journey on foot or in a car. It is easy to get lost in a **white out**—it is impossible to see anything because there is so much snow in the air. Driving is made even more difficult when high winds pile up snow into drifts, which can block roads completely. In countries where heavy snowfall is common, drivers prepare for snow by putting chains on their car wheels to stop them slipping on icy roads. They also carry shovels to clear drifts. However, the dangers of a blizzard are so great that people are usually warned not to go out at all.

▲ In countries where heavy snow is common, people often fix chains over their car tires to help them to grip icy surfaces.

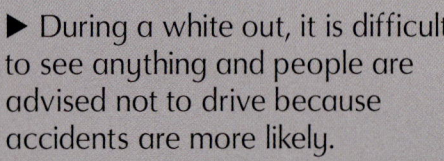

▶ During a white out, it is difficult to see anything and people are advised not to drive because accidents are more likely.

▲ In December 2005, an aircraft skidded off the runway and onto a road in Chicago during a snowstorm.

RAIL, AIR, AND SEA

Railways can be blocked by drifting snow, and the cold temperatures may cause the points—the devices that trains use to change tracks—to become frozen and unusable. Strong winds and snow can make it impossible for aircraft to take off or land, and it is common for airports to be closed. At sea, crews on ships have difficulty seeing anything, while high winds can create huge waves. Freezing water on the upper parts of a small ship can make it top-heavy, causing it to capsize.

▶ Workers repair power lines during the 1998 **ice storm** in Canada.

ICE STORMS

When rain freezes as soon as it touches the ground, it is called an ice storm. In January 1998, one of the worst ice storms ever hit Canada and the northeast of the United States. More than 100,000 people left their homes to find warmth and safety. At least 25 people died, mainly from the cold.

Surviving a blizzard

People who live in places where blizzards are common need to know how to survive while they are cut off from the outside world.

▼ A snow hole is warmer and more comfortable than a tent, and provides better shelter during a blizzard.

STAYING SAFE OUTDOORS

Walkers and climbers should carry cell phones and, if possible, modern **navigation equipment**. Then, if they become trapped, they can tell rescuers where they are. Bright-colored **waterproof** clothing makes them easy to see. If snow is likely, they should not be outdoors but, if they are, it is a good idea to carry a shovel. Then they can dig a small shelter called a **snow hole** for protection until the storm is over and rescuers arrive.

▼ Cars can become completely buried in a snowdrift and have to be dug out.

INDOORS, OR IN A CAR

At home, it is important to stock up with food and drinking water. People need to be able to warm the house without gas or electricity, for example, by having plenty of firewood. Candles are useful, too. It is best to wear many layers of thin clothing to keep warm, and to wear something waterproof when going outside. Drivers who think there may be a risk should carry extra clothing, as well as blankets, food and drink, and a shovel. Anyone who is trapped should tie something brightly colored to the aerial and then stay inside their car.

SURVIVING IN THE SNOW

In 1943, during World War II, Norwegian Resistance fighter Jan Baalsrud fled from the Germans through the Arctic snow of northern Norway. He hid in a snow hole for more than a month before being rescued by local reindeer herders.

▲ Walkers in the snow should wear several layers of clothing to keep warm. These should be waterproof and brightly colored, so they can be easily seen during a rescue.

15

Dangers to health

Cold weather can bring a range of serious health problems. Even indoors, there can be dangers if people are trapped without proper heating and are cut off from sources of help and support.

◀ In cold, snowy weather, ice can settle on the face, especially in hair. The face should be protected with a mask to avoid **frostbite**.

SNOW AND WIND

One of the most serious problems that cold temperatures can bring is **hypothermia**. This is when the body temperature drops to dangerously low levels. If a person's body temperature drops to around 95 degrees Fahrenheit, they may become dizzy and confused. At lower temperatures than that, they become unconscious and eventually die. Older people and babies are at special risk, but anyone trapped in a cold place can be in danger, especially if their clothing is wet. Low temperatures are made worse if there is a wind, as this cools body temperature much more than still air. This effect is called **wind chill**.

FROSTBITE

Extreme cold can cause frostbite—damage to the flesh that most commonly affects the face, fingers, and toes. It starts with the flesh going white and hard because the blood supply is withdrawn to save the body's heat. This causes the sufferer to feel a tingling sensation. The area affected becomes numb, and then red and swollen. Severe frostbite can damage the body so badly that the affected parts may have to be amputated, or removed.

▲ Hands can suffer badly from frostbite. The fingers start to swell and may have to be removed.

TRAGEDY IN THE ANTARCTIC

In 1912, a team of British explorers, led by Captain Robert Falcon Scott, was caught in a blizzard on the way back from the South Pole. Captain Lawrence Oates had severe frostbite and knew he was slowing down the team, so he walked into the blizzard and was never seen again.

▶ Captain Robert Falcon Scott and his team of explorers died in 1912, as they returned from the South Pole.

17

Dealing with snow

Once a blizzard is over, the job of clearing up begins. In countries where heavy snowfall is common, this can be done quickly. If the blizzard is unusually severe, or if it happens where communities are not well prepared, clearing up can take many days.

CLEARING THE ROADS

Special machinery is used to clear roads. Snowploughs can push snow off roads, while snow blowers blow it from the surface, sometimes into a truck, to be taken away. In some countries, salt is spread on roads when snow is **forecast**. Salt brings down the freezing point of water, which helps to prevent ice from forming. Grit and sand can be spread on icy roads to stop tires slipping.

▶ A snowplough clears a road. In places where snow is common, these machines are kept on standby throughout winter.

▶ A **meteorologist** checks the depth of snow using an instrument called a **snow gauge**.

BE PREPARED

Accurate weather forecasts can save lives. If people know that a blizzard is on its way, they can stay indoors and stock up with food and fuel. Walkers and climbers can stay off the hills and mountains, and farmers can bring their animals in before the storms are at their worst.

▼ In parts of the world that often get heavy snowfall, people may have small snow blowers to clear pathways.

RESCUE SERVICES

After a heavy blizzard, people in isolated communities may be cut off from the outside world. Rescue organizations may have to drop food and medical supplies and airlift people to safety. Search and rescue teams once used dogs to try to find people trapped under heavy snow, and farmers still use dogs to find trapped livestock. Today, rescue helicopters can be fitted with **heat-sensitive cameras**, which can detect warm bodies trapped under the snow.

▶ When roads are blocked, the only way to reach someone who is sick or injured may be by helicopter.

Plants and animals

Plants and animals that naturally live in cold climates have developed a range of ways to live through harsh weather.

DRESSING FOR WINTER

In winter, the coat of many hunters, such as the Arctic fox, change to white, so they can hunt in the snow without being seen. Animals that are hunted, such as the Arctic hare, also have white coats to make them difficult to see.

HIBERNATION

Some animals avoid cold winters by **migrating** to somewhere warmer. A few creatures **hibernate**—they hide away and go into a very deep kind of sleep, when their body temperature drops and their heartbeat slows. Others, such as bears, get as fat as possible in fall, then find somewhere cozy to stay until warmer weather comes.

▲ Polar bear mothers spend winter in a den in the snow. Their cubs are born there and come outside in spring.

◀ Emperor penguin parents use their bodies to protect their young from the bitterly cold Antarctic temperatures.

KEEPING WARM

Male Emperor penguins also build up stores of body fat, but they do not sleep. Instead, they spend the Antarctic winter looking after their eggs in temperatures as low as -40 degrees Fahrenheit, huddling together for warmth. In the Arctic, creatures such as musk oxen must live through the cold weather. They rely on thick fur to protect them from the cold, and know how to find grass beneath the snow. For lemmings and other small creatures, the snow provides shelter and they live safely underneath it. Farm animals, however, do not have the **adaptations** they need. Young animals are in danger of being buried in drifts, and can die from the cold and lack of food.

PLANT LIFE

The **cells** that make up a plant's stems or leaves can be damaged if they freeze. Some plants that grow in cold climates contain special chemicals that do not easily freeze. This allows the plants to live through very low temperatures. The pointed shape of fir and pine trees causes snow to slide off the branches, so they do not break under the weight of the snow.

▼ The branches of fir trees slope downward. This allows snow to slip off. If the branches were straight, they would break easily.

Living with snow

In some of the coldest parts of the world, people have known for centuries how to live through cold, snowy weather.

THE INUIT PEOPLE

Inuit is the name for several groups of people who traditionally live in the far north, close to the Arctic, in Canada, Alaska, Russia, and Greenland. Today, many Inuits live in modern houses, but some still follow the traditional way of life. They hunt and fish using spears and **harpoons**, travel on sleds drawn by husky dogs, and dress in reindeer furs.

▲ The igloo is made from blocks of snow and is warm inside, even in the coldest winter weather.

IGLOOS

Some Inuit build traditional snow houses called **igloos**. Often, these are temporary homes, built quickly from blocks of snow and used during hunting trips. They provide shelter from extremely low temperatures and harsh, Arctic winter winds.

▼ People of the Arctic regions still use sleds, pulled by husky dogs, to cross the ice and snow.

▼ The **Sami** live in the far north of Scandinavia, where winters are harsh. The reindeer survive on a diet of lichens, which they find under the snow.

THE SAMI AND THEIR REINDEER

The Sami people live in northern Scandinavia, where winters are bitterly cold. Reindeer are well suited to these conditions. The Sami have traditionally relied on them for skin, milk, and meat, and as a means of transport.

THE ROOF OF THE WORLD

The country of Tibet lies among the mountains of Asia. This region is so high up that it is often called the "roof of the world." At this altitude, winters are harsh. Traditional houses are built with thick walls to keep out the cold. The kitchens and the cattle's stalls are on the ground floor. During the coldest months, the cattle are kept in these stalls and the heat from their bodies, as well as from the cooking stove, rises and warms the living space above.

▲ A ger is the traditional felt tent used by the **nomads** of the high Mongolia plateau in Asia. Gers provide warm shelter, even in the cold winter.

23

Blizzard tales

Some blizzards are so severe, or do such great damage, that people remember them for many years.

THE GREAT SNOW

Four blizzards in New England between February and March 1717 became known as the Great Snow. There were drifts more than 24 feet deep. It was said that people could step out onto snow from their first-floor windows. Thousands of cattle and sheep died. More recently, severe blizzards hit the United States in 1978—in Ohio and New England. Near the coast, the storm happened at the same time as high tides, bringing floods along with snow and causing around $500 million worth of damage in Massachusetts alone.

THE SNOW QUEEN

The children's story, *The Snow Queen* is by Hans Christian Andersen. It tells of a boy, Kay, who is taken by a magical Snow Queen during a blizzard to her ice palace in the far north. He is rescued through the love of a young girl, Gerda.

▲ The Snow Queen appears in a blizzard to a boy named Kay—and kidnaps him.

◄ A blizzard in 1978 struck the northeast of the United States, covering New York City in snow.

BRITAIN, 1947

In Britain, between January and March 1947, there was unusually heavy snow, with high winds. When it finally melted, there was also heavy rain and severe floods. The winter of 1962–1963 in Britain was actually much colder than 1947—it was the coldest for more than 200 years. However, it was not as snowy.

GENERAL WINTER DEFEATS NAPOLEON

Blizzards in Russia in the winter of 1812–1813 changed the course of history. A French invading army of several hundred thousand, led by Napoleon, reached Moscow, Russia, but was forced to retreat during a series of blizzards. Only around 10,000 soldiers made it back to France. The Russians said that Napoleon had been defeated by two great soldiers—General Starvation and General Winter.

▶ Soldiers of the French army trudge through the snow as they return from Moscow, Russia, in 1813.

▲ In 1947, the Royal Air Force prepared bread to be dropped to villages in Britain that were completely cut off due to heavy snow.

Coping with blizzards

No one can stop blizzards happening, but we can make sure our homes stay warm and safe, and there are modern ways to travel in snowy places.

▼ Crowds outside the Knickerbocker Theater, Washington D.C., in 1922. The snowstorm that brought its roof down became known as the "Knickerbocker Storm."

COLLAPSING ROOFS

In 1922, so much snow piled up on the roof of the Knickerbocker Theater, Washington D.C., that it fell in—killing 98 people and injuring 133. A similar accident happened in Poland in 2006, when the roof of a trade hall in Katowice collapsed, killing 66 people and injuring 150.

▲ Houses in the Alps have steep roofs, so that snow will not pile up.

BUILDING FOR COLD WEATHER

Buildings can be built to last during cold weather and heavy snow. Sometimes, ideas developed in the past are still used. For example, houses in the Alps have always had steeply pitched roofs, allowing snow to slide off easily. Homes can be well insulated. Materials that work like thick blankets are put into the walls and under the roof to keep the warmth inside, and to keep the cold out. Windows can be double- or even triple-glazed, which means having two or three panes of glass in them. This helps to stop heat from escaping. In some countries, such as Canada, there are whole streets of shops built underground, away from harsh winter weather.

KEEPING IN TOUCH IN THE SNOW

Isolated settlements can use radio communications to keep in touch with the outside world, even when power and telephone lines are down. Where heavy snow is common, people use sleds to get around, often pulled by dogs. They can also use **snowmobiles**— motor vehicles that travel on skis. There are even aircraft that can take off and land using skis.

◀ Snowmobiles can travel up to 50 miles an hour. They are used both for travel and sport.

The changing climate

On average, temperatures around the world are getting warmer. Called **global warming**, it is causing changes in climate and could mean that extreme weather conditions happen more often.

PAST AND PRESENT

In the past, the Earth's climate has been both warmer and cooler than today. It is now getting warmer—very fast. Most scientists believe that humans are causing this. We are burning huge amounts of **fossil fuels**—coal, oil, and gas—creating **carbon dioxide** gas, which warms the Earth's atmosphere. Green plants absorb carbon dioxide, but we are destroying forests, which has made the situation worse.

▼ As the Earth's climate gets warmer, the ice in the seas around the Arctic and Antarctic will break up.

Sun's rays
Sun's rays are reflected
Heat escapes
Sun's rays are trapped, which warms the atmosphere

▲ The Sun warms the Earth and certain gases, such as carbon dioxide, trap some of the heat in the atmosphere. They act like the glass in a greenhouse.

THE FUTURE

Scientists report that winters in the Arctic and Antarctic have been warmer in recent years, and much of the ice that covers large areas of the land and sea has begun to melt. There is also less snow on some mountains, such as Kilimanjaro in Tanzania. No one really knows what weather patterns climate change will bring. Some places may get more extreme storms and blizzards, while regions that used to have snow regularly may no longer get any. However, scientists agree that, on average, temperatures over the world will continue to rise.

THE GREENHOUSE EFFECT

When the Sun heats the Earth's surface, this warms the air above it. **Greenhouse gases**, such as carbon dioxide, trap this heat. This is called the **greenhouse effect**—and causes the Earth to become warmer.

▲ Global warming does not always mean less snow. Record snowfall in New York in 2006 meant it was possible to ski in the city.

Glossary

ADAPTATION
A change to suit the environment or a way of life.

ALTITUDE
The height of a place above sea level.

ANTARCTIC
The region around the South Pole.

ARCTIC
The region around the North Pole.

ATMOSPHERE
The blanket of air around the Earth.

CARBON DIOXIDE
One of the gases in the air. Carbon dioxide is also produced when fuel is burned.

CELL
The smallest part of a living thing.

CONDENSE
To change from a gas into a liquid.

CRYSTAL
A clear, regularly-shaped solid.

DENDRITE
A branched crystal—six-sided snowflakes are called dendrites.

DRIFT
Snow heaped up by the wind.

FORECAST
To predict the future, such as the weather.

FOSSIL FUELS
Coal, oil, and natural gas. These fuels were formed millions of years ago from the remains of plants and marine animals.

FROSTBITE
The damage caused to parts of the body by exposure to severe cold.

GLOBAL WARMING
Increase in the average temperature of the air around the Earth. Global warming is caused by an increase in greenhouse gases, such as carbon dioxide, in the air.

GREENHOUSE EFFECT
The way that greenhouse gases trap warm air close to the Earth's surface.

GREENHOUSE GAS
One of the gases in the air that trap the Sun's heat. Greenhouse gases include water vapor, carbon dioxide, and methane.

HARPOON
A kind of spear with a rope tied to it, used for fishing and catching whales.

HEAT-SENSITIVE CAMERA
A camera that detects the amount of heat given off from objects and then shows this as pictures. Also called a thermograph.

HIBERNATE
A kind of sleep that is very close to death, when the body temperature drops and breathing and the heartbeat almost stop.

HYPOTHERMIA
When the body's temperature drops dangerously low.

ICE STORM
Freezing rain that covers everything with a layer of ice.

IGLOO
A traditional type of house made from snow by the Inuit people.

INUIT
A group of native people who traditionally live in the Arctic regions of the world.

METEOROLOGIST
A scientist who studies the weather.

MIGRATE
To move to another place. In animals, this means to travel from one place to another with the change in seasons.

NAVIGATION EQUIPMENT
Instruments used by ships and aircraft to help them to find out their position and route.

NOMAD
A wanderer. Some groups of people are traditionally "nomadic" because they spend their lives moving from place to place. For example, across grasslands or deserts, with their livestock.

PERMANENT SNOW LINE
The point on a mountain above which there is always snow.

PLATEAU
A flat area of high land.

POWER LINE
A heavy wire for carrying electricity.

SAMI
A group of people who traditionally live in northern Scandinavia, northern Europe.

SEA LEVEL
The level of the surface of the sea.

SNOW GAUGE
A scientific instrument for measuring how much snow has fallen.

SNOW HOLE
A cave dug out of the snow.

SNOWMOBILE
A motor vehicle with skis for traveling across the snow.

TROPICS
Part of the world on each side of the Equator between the Tropic of Cancer and the Tropic of Capricorn.

WATERPROOF
When water cannot pass through.

WATER VAPOR
Water in the form of a gas.

WHITE OUT
Snow in the air that is so thick, it is impossible to see through it.

WIND CHILL
The combined cooling effect of wind and cold temperatures.

Index

altitude 8, 10, 11, 23
animals 19, 20–21
Antarctic 8, 17, 21, 29
Arctic 9, 22, 29
atmosphere 6, 28
avalanches 10, 11

body fat 20, 21
body temperature 16, 20
buildings 26, 27

carbon dioxide 28, 29
climate change 28–29
clothing 14, 15
clouds 6, 7
communications 27

easterly winds 9
explorers 17

fir trees 21
frostbite 16, 17
fur 21

ger 23
global warming 28, 29
greenhouse gases 28, 29

health 16–17
heat-sensitive cameras 19
helicopters 19
hibernation 20
houses 22, 23
hypothermia 16

ice 16, 22, 28, 29
ice crystals 6, 7
ice storm 13
icy roads 12
igloos 22
insulation 27
Inuit people 22, 27

migration 20
mountains 10–11, 19, 29
musk oxen 9, 21

navigation equipment 14

pack ice 28
penguins 8, 21
permanent snow line 11
pine trees 21
plants 20-21, 28
polar bears 20
polar regions 7, 11
poles 9, 17
power lines 12, 13

railways 13
reindeer 22, 23
rescue 14, 15, 19
roads 4, 18, 19, 27

Sami people 23
sleds 22, 27
snow cave 14, 15
snow gauge 18
snow houses (igloos) 22

snowdrifts 4, 12, 15, 21, 24
snowfall 9, 12, 18, 19
snowflakes 6, 7
snowmobiles 27
snowploughs 18
snowstorms 4, 5
survival 14–15

traveling 4, 12
tropical regions 11

water vapor 6, 9
waves 13
weather forecasts 19
westerly winds 9
white out 12
wind chill 16